TINY BITES

Scratch Recipes
for the Toy Oven

Susan Berry Eberhardt

Epigraph Books
Rhinebeck, New York

D1404268

Cover and book design by Daria Erdosy
Photography by Susan Berry Eberhardt

Library of Congress Control Number: 2015953163
ISBN: 978-1-944037-08-6

Epigraph Publishing Service
22 East Market Street, Suite 304
Rhinebeck, NY 12572
www.epigraphps.com

Printed in the United States of America

For my grandchildren

contents

WOW! **You got a toy oven for your birthday, Christmas or another occasion — cool!** I'll bet you used up the mix that came with it on the very first day. Now what? You could go to the toy store to buy more mixes — not very convenient. You could order some online, but it would take a long time for the stuff to arrive in the mail. You could do what my daughter did: make up your own concoctions and offer rock-hard salty cookies to your family. Or, you could make yummy treats with the recipes in this book using ingredients your family probably already has in the cabinet and refrigerator.

If you are careful to measure accurately and bake for the right amount of time, you will make cookies and cakes that are more delicious than the ones from the mixes, a whole lot less expensive and more natural, too.

You will also learn a lot about baking. Some recipes are marked, "Super Easy!" If you are a beginner cook, you might want to start with these, then try the more complicated ones.

Happy baking and happy eating!

TOY OVENS THROUGH THE YEARS

Kids have enjoyed cooking for centuries. The first stove in the picture is a wood stove. It was probably made as a salesman's model, not a toy, but kids played with stoves like these years ago, making real wood fires inside. Did any houses burn down because of their play?

The electric stove on the right was a popular toy in the 1920s and 1930s. The author's mother got one for Christmas when she was five years old. You can cook on top of the stove as well as in the oven — and you can really burn yourself!

The white stove was made in the 1950s. You can cook on top of that one, too. More burned fingers?

The Kenner Company designed the safety-minded Easy-Bake oven in 1963 and sold half a million ovens that year. It looked like the turquoise one in the picture and used two light bulbs. Over time this oven (and others, like the Holly Hobbie) went through several transformations. For a while, Easy-Bake was owned by General Mills, who also made Betty Crocker cake mixes for it. For most of its existence, it used one light bulb for heat. Now produced by the Hasbro toy company, it has a heating element inside—no more light bulb.

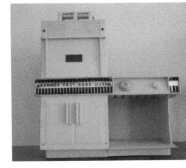

After so many years and so many ovens sold, there must be millions sitting in attics and closets all over the country. Let's get them out and start baking!

7

SaFeTY

Be clean
If you don't wash your hands before cooking, nobody will want to eat what you cook (and you shouldn't eat it either). You also need to wash your hands after handling raw meat. Make sure all of your utensils are clean.

Don't cut yourself
Ask your parents for permission when you need to use a sharp knife or the grater, and ask them to show you the safe way to do it. (No blood in the dough, please.)

Don't get burned
Use the pan holder that came with your oven and remember that the pan is very hot after you've baked something. If you are cooking in a toaster oven or regular oven, hot pads can help you get the pan out safely.

Don't get sick
Raw egg can have germs in it, so don't eat the raw dough or lick the bowl. Cooking kills the germs. Cakes coming out of the Easy-Bake oven reach 160°F, the recommended temperature for eggs.

EQUIPMENT

Ovens

These recipes were developed and tested in two light bulb ovens and the new Easy-Bake Ultimate Oven. Be sure to preheat the oven for 20 minutes before you bake. If, when you try the first recipe, your results are under-baked or over-baked, you should adjust the cooking time in all the recipes. There's no way to check on baking progress while the cake is in the toy oven and it's often impossible to put it back in the oven if it's underdone.

The recipes were also tested in a toaster oven at 350° on the "bake" setting. The same baking times should work in any toaster oven or regular oven, but if you don't get the expected results, adjust the times. At least, with these ovens you can check on the cake's progress and replace it if necessary.

Pans

All the recipes are designed for the standard pans that come with toy ovens: a round one 3 ½" in diameter or a rectangular one 5¾" x 3¾". Be careful not to fill the pans too full.

Some recipes were tested with muffins pans. The light bulb oven has a muffin pan with four cups; the Ultimate oven has a six-cup muffin pan. In general, you need to cut the regular recipe in half to make **cupcakes or muffins**. (Use a recipe for cake or one of the quick breads: corn, blueberry or banana nut..)

Plastic Ice Cube Tray:

Use this to freeze eggs in recipe-sized portions. The instructions for its use are given under "Your Ingredients" on page 11.

Like a Volcano

Have you ever seen a model volcano at a science fair? You can make a model of a volcano out of clay, papier-mâché or even dirt, then put some baking soda in the hollow. (Or just use a glass with a teaspoon of baking soda in it.) Pour in some vinegar and foam will come out and run down the sides of the mountain just like lava. **Baking soda** is a base (alkali) and **vinegar** is an acid. When they get together they react, creating lots of bubbles. Someone figured out they could use this reaction to make nice, fluffy cakes.

Baking powder is even more convenient because it contains both baking soda and an acid, which only need a liquid to create the reaction. (You can try this, too: put a teaspoon of baking powder in a glass, add a little water and watch what happens.)

This book contains some recipes that use baking soda with an acid (like fruit juice, yogurt or molasses) and some that use baking powder.

Another way to make dough fluffy is with **yeast**. Yeast is lots of tiny organisms that like sugar. When you put yeast in your dough, it eats the sugar and creates bubbles, so your dough will puff up. The yeast recipes in this book are not difficult but they take a long time. Yeast doesn't like to be rushed!

You can also use **egg whites** to make your cakes rise. When you beat egg whites, you beat air into them, making — yes — bubbles. There are no recipes in this book using egg whites because these cakes would rise too high and get stuck in your toy oven. For a full-size recipe using egg whites look in a cookbook or online for angel food cake, sponge cake or meringue.

YᴏUR INGREDIENTS

Egg chips: It's hard to find teeny-weeny eggs for toy-sized recipes. Do you have a pet lovebird? In case you don't, and your parents won't let you throw out most of a chicken egg after you use what you want for your recipe, here's the solution: spray a plastic ice cube tray with non-stick spray. In a small bowl, beat a large egg well with a fork until it's all one color. Measure one teaspoon of the egg into each compartment of the ice cube tray. Cover and set on a level place in the freezer. When they're frozen you can pop them out and keep them in a plastic bag in the freezer.

To thaw, take the number of egg chips you need and place them on a small plate on top of the heated toy oven until they begin to soften (about 1-2 minutes depending on the thickness of your plate). Then mash with a fork until they are completely liquefied. Be careful: egg chips thaw quickly, so put the unused ones back in the freezer right away.

Flour: Many of these recipes specify self-rising flour. You can substitute all-purpose flour or cake flour if you add a dash of baking powder and a speck of salt for each tablespoon of flour and mix very well.

Complete pancake mix: Use the kind that contains shortening and powdered milk. The instructions on the box should say you only need to add water to make pancakes.

11

MeasuRing & Clean UP

Measuring:

For these recipes, you don't need to sift the flour. Just scoop it up in the measuring spoon and level it off with a knife. The same goes for all dry ingredients except brown sugar, which should be packed down in the spoon — use the flat side of a table knife to squish as much brown sugar as you can into the spoon and level it off.

For butter, cream cheese and shortening, don't rely on the markings on the wrapper. Squish the stuff into a measuring spoon and level it off with a knife.

When you are measuring, hold the spoon over the sink with your mixing bowl on the counter next to you. If you measure over your bowl and spill something, you will ruin your recipe. Measure dry ingredients before wet ones.

To measure a drop of vanilla, pour it into the cap before you add it to your other ingredients.

In this book, small measurements are:

Dash = 1/8 teaspoon = size of a peanut
Pinch = 1/16 teaspoon = size of a chocolate chip
Smidgen or drop = 1/32 teaspoon = size of half a pea
Speck = the amount you can pick up on the end of a flat toothpick

They make measuring spoons in these small amounts. If you have them, you'll find them handy.

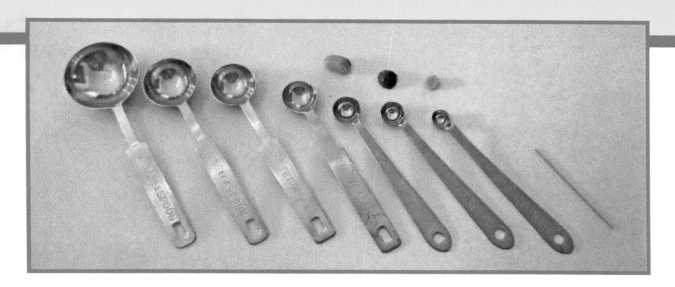

Clean Up:

The pans that come with toy ovens need to be hand-washed and dried, not put in the dishwasher.

Wipe up any spills right away. When they dry they are harder to deal with. Besides, if you spill something on the floor, it could be slippery.

You should wash your utensils and straighten up the kitchen right after you've finished cooking. Your family will let you use the kitchen more often if you don't leave everything in a mess.

oatmeal Bar cookies

super easy!

Round pan:

- 1 tablespoon complete pancake mix
- 1 tablespoon quick-cooking oatmeal
- 1 tablespoon sugar
- 1 smidgen cinnamon
- 1 teaspoon raisins
- 1 tablespoon water

Rectangular pan:

- 2 tablespoons complete pancake mix
- 2 tablespoons quick-cooking oatmeal
- 2 tablespoons sugar
- ¼ teaspoon cinnamon
- 2 teaspoons raisins
- 2 tablespoons water

Preheat the oven and butter the pan. Mix all ingredients together and spread in pan.

Bake 20 minutes.

When cooled, cut into bars.

BROWNIES

SUPER EASY!

Round pan

2 teaspoons butter
2 teaspoons unsweetened
   cocoa
2 tablespoons sugar
2 egg chips
1 drop vanilla
1 speck salt
1 tablespoon all-purpose flour

Rectangular pan

4 teaspoons butter
1 tablespoon unsweetened
   cocoa
3 tablespoons sugar
3 egg chips
1 drop vanilla
1 speck salt
3 tablespoons all-purpose flour

Preheat the oven; butter the pan.

Put the butter in your mixing bowl
and set on top of the oven to melt.
Stir cocoa into melted butter.
Add sugar, then eggs, vanilla and salt.
Stir in flour.

Spread evenly in pan.

Bake 20 minutes.

When cooled, cut into bars.

Tip:
Replace unused egg chips to the
freezer right away. They thaw very
quickly.

BLONDIES

SUPER EASY!

Round pan

2 teaspoons butter
2 tablespoons sugar
2 egg chips
1 drop vanilla
1 speck salt
2 tablespoons all-purpose flour

Rectangular pan

1 tablespoon butter
3 tablespoons sugar
3 egg chips
1 drop vanilla
1 speck salt
3 tablespoons all-purpose flour

Preheat the oven and butter the pan.

Put the butter in your mixing bowl and set on top of the oven to melt.

Add sugar to melted butter. Stir in eggs, vanilla and salt. Mix in flour. Spread evenly in pan.

Bake 20 minutes.

When cooled, cut into bars.

PENUCHE BARS

Use the blondies recipe but use brown sugar instead of white.

17

Vanilla & Chocolate
Drop Cookies

Vanilla

1 teaspoon butter
1 tablespoon sugar (white or brown)
1 egg chip
1 drop vanilla
1 teaspoon milk
2 tablespoons self-rising flour

Preheat oven and butter the pan. Cream butter and sugar together, mix in thawed egg chip, vanilla and milk. Add flour and mix well, mashing the mixture against the bowl with the back of the spoon.

Chocolate

1¼ teaspoons butter
1 tablespoon sugar
1 teaspoon unsweetened cocoa
1 egg chip
1 teaspoon milk
1 drop vanilla
2 tablespoons self-rising flour

Preheat oven and butter the pan. Cream butter and sugar together. Add the cocoa and mix well. Add thawed egg chip, milk and vanilla. Stir in the flour.

Baking instructions for both:

Measure ½ teaspoon dough and drop into pan, pushing it out with another spoon or a table knife. Arrange 6 dough blobs in the round pan or 12 blobs in the rectangular pan. Press down with your finger to flatten them a bit. Bake 8 minutes.

Oatmeal Drop Cookies

4 teaspoons all-purpose flour
1 smidgen salt
1 smidgen baking soda
1 smidgen cinnamon
1 tablespoon brown sugar
1 tablespoon white sugar
1 tablespoon butter
2 egg chips
1 drop vanilla
2 tablespoons quick-cooking oats
1 tablespoon raisins
1 tablespoon chopped pecans
    or walnuts

Preheat oven; butter the pan.

In a small bowl, mix flour, salt, baking soda and cinnamon together.

In your mixing bowl, cream both sugars and butter together well. Add eggs and vanilla. Stir in flour and then oats. Add raisins and nuts.

Measure ½ teaspoon of dough and scrape off spoon into pan. Repeat, placing 5 blobs of dough evenly spaced in the round pan or 10 blobs in the rectangular pan. Bake 10 minutes.

Repeat baking until dough is used up.

TOLL HOUSE COOKIES

2 tablespoons all-purpose flour
1 pinch baking soda
1 pinch salt
1 tablespoon butter
2 teaspoons brown sugar
2 teaspoons white sugar
1 drop vanilla
2 egg chips
4 teaspoons chocolate chips
2 teaspoons chopped pecans

Preheat the oven and butter the pan.

Mix the flour, baking soda and salt in a small bowl. In a different bowl, cream the butter and sugars together, then add the egg and vanilla to the butter mixture and beat one minute. Add the flour and mix well. Stir in the chocolate chips and pecans.

Using your ½ teaspoon measuring spoon, take a blob of dough and place it in the pan. You can fit 4 blobs in the round pan and 8 blobs in the rectangular pan. Press each blob down with your fingers so it doesn't rise above the rim of the pan. Bake 11 minutes.

Repeat baking until all the dough is used.

Makes about 16 cookies.

Peanut Butter Cookies

These are a little different from other drop cookies because you roll them into balls before putting them in the pan.

1½ tablespoons all-purpose flour
1 dash teaspoon baking soda
2 teaspoons soft butter
2 teaspoons brown sugar
2 teaspoons white sugar
1 drop vanilla
1 egg chip
1 tablespoon smooth peanut
    butter

Preheat the oven; butter the pan. Mix the flour and baking soda together very well. Mix all the other ingredients in another bowl, then combine the two mixtures.

Using ½ teaspoon of the dough, make into a ball with your hands.

Put 4 balls in the round pan and 8 balls in the rectangular pan.

Flatten each dough ball with a fork, leaving an impression of the tines in the dough. Bake 13 minutes. Repeat until all the dough is used — about 16 cookies.

Vanilla & Chocolate SLiCED COOKieS

Vanilla

2 teaspoons soft butter

1 tablespoon sugar

1 egg chip

1 drop vanilla

4 teaspoons self-rising flour

Cream butter and sugar together. Add egg and vanilla and mix well. Mix in flour.

Chocolate

2 teaspoons soft butter

1 tablespoon sugar

1 egg chip

1 drop vanilla

½ teaspoon unsweetened cocoa

4 teaspoons self-rising flour

Cream butter and sugar together. Add egg, vanilla and cocoa and mix well. Mix in flour.

Baking Sliced Cookies

Preheat oven. Butter the pan. Make either the vanilla or chocolate dough.

With your hands, form the dough into a cylinder about the diameter of a nickel. Wrap in wax paper or plastic wrap and refrigerate at least one hour.

When dough is chilled, cut slices the thickness of a nickel: 5 for the round pan or 12 for the rectangular pan. Arrange in pan. Decorate with sprinkles if desired. Replace unused dough in refrigerator.

Bake 8 minutes. Repeat, slicing and baking until all the dough is used.

"WHAT'S THAT...?"

CREAM THE BUTTER:

With the back of a spoon, squish the butter against the bowl until it is soft and creamy.

PiNWHEEL COOKieS

Half a batch of vanilla sliced cookie dough and half a batch of chocolate sliced cookie dough, page 22.

Make the vanilla dough and chocolate dough in separate bowls. Sprinkle a little flour on a piece of wax paper and on your hands. With your hands, pat the vanilla dough onto the wax paper into a rectangle 4 inches by 1½ inches. On another piece of wax paper, do the same with the chocolate dough. Place the chocolate dough

on top of the vanilla (paper side up) and press the two rectangles of dough together. Carefully remove the top piece of wax paper.

Now, roll up the dough into a cylinder. You might need a spatula to unstick the dough from the wax paper under it. Pat it into an even cylinder, wrap in wax paper and refrigerate at least an hour.

Slice and bake according to the instructions on page 22.

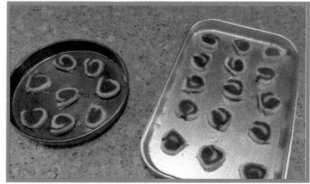

24

CHEESE WAFERS

And now something not so sweet.

1 tablespoon soft butter
1 tablespoon shredded
    cheddar cheese
3 tablespoons all-purpose flour
1 smidgen salt

Preheat oven and butter the pan.

Mix butter and cheese together.
Add flour and salt and mix well.
Form into a cylinder, chill, and
cut as for refrigerator cookies,
page 22.

Bake 8 minutes.

Peach Cobbler

Round Pan

1 teaspoon butter
1 tablespoon sugar
4½ teaspoons self-rising flour
4½ teaspoons peach juice or milk
Enough diced peaches to cover the
    bottom of the pan
(canned or fresh; if you use canned,
drain well and save the juice)
1 smidgen nutmeg

Rectangular Pan

2 teaspoons butter
4½ teaspoons sugar
2 tablespoons self-rising flour
2 tablespoons peach juice or milk
Enough diced peaches to cover the
    bottom of the pan
(canned or fresh; if you use canned,
drain well and save the juice)
1 pinch nutmeg

Preheat oven.

Put butter in pan and set on top of oven to melt.

Mix flour and sugar. Add melted butter and juice or milk; mix well. Arrange peaches in pan and sprinkle with nutmeg. Pour batter on top and spread out. Bake 30 minutes.

Variations: Use blueberries or apples with cinnamon.

COFFEE CAKE

Round Pan

2 tablespoons self-rising cake flour
1 tablespoon sugar
1 pinch cinnamon
1 teaspoon soft butter
1 egg chip
4½ teaspoons milk
1 teaspoon raisins
1 teaspoon chopped pecans

Rectangular Pan

3 tablespoons self-rising cake flour
1 tablespoon sugar
1 teaspoon soft butter
1 pinch cinnamon
1 egg chip
2 tablespoons milk
2 teaspoons raisins
2 teaspoons chopped pecans

Preheat your oven and butter the pan.

Mix flour, sugar and cinnamon. Add soft butter and mash it into the dry ingredients with a fork. Add egg and milk and beat until completely mixed. Add raisins and nuts.

Bake 25 minutes.

Frost with cream cheese frosting, page 40, or drizzle cookie glaze on top, page 41.

CORN BREAD

Round pan

1 tablespoon cornmeal
1 tablespoon all-purpose flour
1½ teaspoons sugar
¼ teaspoon baking powder
1 smidgen salt
2 teaspoons melted
2 egg chips
2½ teaspoons milk

Rectangular pan

4½ teaspoons cornmeal
4½ teaspoons all-purpose flour
1 tablespoon sugar
¼ teaspoon baking powder
1 pinch salt
3 teaspoons melted butter
3 egg chips
2 tablespoons milk

Preheat oven, butter pan.

Mix dry ingredients together thoroughly. (A fork does a good job.) Beat eggs, melted butter and milk together, then add wet mixture to dry mixture.

Spread evenly in pan.

Bake 20 minutes.

BLUEBERRY BREAD

Round Pan:

1 teaspoon butter
6 blueberries
2 tablespoons self-rising flour
2 teaspoons sugar
1 egg chip, thawed
1 tablespoon milk

Rectangular Pan:

1½ teaspoons butter
12 blueberries
3 tablespoons self-rising flour
3 teaspoons sugar
2 egg chips, thawed
5 teaspoons milk

Preheat oven and butter the pan.

Put the butter in a bowl and set on top of the oven to melt.

Put the blueberries on a plate and cut each in half.

In a separate bowl, mix the flour and sugar together. Add the egg and milk to the melted butter. Stir the liquid ingredients into the dry. As soon as they are thoroughly combined, spread in the pan. Arrange the blueberries on the batter with the skin side up and poke them down into the batter.

Bake 20 minutes.

29

Banana Nut Bread

Round Pan

1 teaspoon butter
1½ tablespoons self-rising
    cake flour
2 teaspoons sugar
1 egg chip
1½ tablespoons mashed banana
1 tablespoon chopped pecans
    or walnuts

Rectangular Pan

2 teaspoons butter
2 tablespoons self-rising cake flour
3 teaspoons sugar
2 egg chips
2 tablespoons mashed banana
1½ tablespoons chopped pecans
    or walnuts

Preheat oven; butter and flour
the pan.

Put the butter in a bowl and set on
top of the oven to melt.

In a separate bowl, mix the flour and
sugar together. Add the egg and
banana to the melted butter. Mix wet
and dry ingredients together; add
chopped nuts. Spread evenly in pan.

Bake 25 minutes.

vanilla cake

Round pan

1 teaspoon butter at room temp
1 tablespoon sugar
1 egg chip
1 drop vanilla
1½ tablespoons self-rising flour
1½ tablespoons milk

Rectangular pan

2 teaspoons butter at room temp
2 tablespoons sugar
2 egg chips
1 drop vanilla
3 tablespoons self-rising flour
3 tablespoons milk

Preheat oven; butter pan and sprinkle flour in it (or spray with baking spray with flour in it).

Cream butter and sugar together. Add egg and vanilla; beat for one minute with a fork. Add milk and flour and beat one more minute. Pour into pan, tilting pan to spread batter evenly.

Bake 25 minutes

If you like, you can cut the rectangular cake in half to make two layers.

You'll find frosting recipes on page 40.

"WHAT'S THAT...?"
BUTTER AND FLOUR THE PAN:
After buttering the pan, sprinkle some flour on it and shake it around so it forms an even film

CHOCOLATE CAKE

Round pan

1 teaspoon unsweetened cocoa
1½ tablespoons self-rising cake flour
1½ teaspoons butter
1 tablespoon sugar
2 egg chips
1 tablespoon milk
1 drop vanilla

Rectangular pan

1½ teaspoons unsweetened cocoa
1½ tablespoons self-rising flour
2 teaspoons butter
3 egg chips
1½ tablespoons milk
2 drops vanilla
1½ tablespoons milk

Preheat oven; butter and flour the pan

Mix flour and cocoa together a small bowl.

In another bowl, cream the butter and sugar together. Add eggs, milk and vanilla. Add the flour mixture, combine well, and beat one minute.

Bake 20 minutes.

You'll find frosting recipes on page 40.

Tip: There are different ways to tell if a cake is done: the sides of the cake have pulled away from the pan a little; if you touch the middle of the cake, it springs back; a toothpick stuck into it comes out clean.

carrot cake

Round Pan

1 tablespoon all-purpose flour
1 tablespoon sugar
1 pinch cinnamon
1 pinch baking soda
1 speck salt
2 teaspoons vegetable oil
2 egg chips
1 ½ tablespoons grated carrots
1 teaspoon chopped walnuts
    (or other nuts)
1 teaspoon raisins

Rectangular Pan

2 tablespoons all-purpose flour
2 tablespoons sugar
¼ teaspoon cinnamon
1 dash baking soda
1 smidgen salt
4 teaspoons vegetable oil
4 egg chips

3 tablespoons grated carrots
2 teaspoons chopped walnuts
    (or other nuts)
2 teaspoons raisins

Preheat oven; butter and flour pan.

Combine dry ingredients and mix. Mix in oil, egg chips and grated carrots, beat one minute with a fork. Add nuts and raisins.

Bake 25 minutes.

Delicious with cream cheese frosting, page 40

Tip: Use a large piece of carrot to keep your fingers away from the grater. Careful!

Pineapple UPSiDe-DoWn cake

Round Pan

2 teaspoons butter
  (1 in mixing bowl, 1 in pan)
2 egg chips
2 pineapple chunks
1 maraschino cherry
½ tablespoon brown sugar
½ tablespoon pineapple juice
1 tablespoon white sugar
1 tablespoon self-rising flour

Rectangular Pan

3½ teaspoons butter
  (2 in mixing bowl, 1½ in pan)
3 egg chips
4 pineapple chunks
2 maraschino cherries
1 tablespoon brown sugar
¾ tablespoon pineapple juice
1½ tablespoons white sugar
1½ tablespoons self-rising flour

Set baking pan and mixing bowl on top of oven to melt butter.

Cut fruit into small pieces.

When butter in baking pan is melted, add the brown sugar and mix, spreading mixture evenly in bottom of pan. Arrange fruit on top.

Mix white sugar and juice with butter in bowl, then add thawed egg chips. Beat with a fork. Add flour and beat again.

Pour batter evenly into baking pan without moving the fruit around. Bake 15 minutes.

When the pan is cool enough to touch, run a knife around the edge of the cake, then put a plate on top. Turn the pan and plate over so the cake comes out onto the plate.

ReD Velvet cake

Round Pan

¼ teaspoon unsweetened cocoa
½ teaspoon red food color
2 tablespoons cake flour
   (not self-rising)
1 smidgen salt
1 pinch baking soda
2 teaspoons butter
1 tablespoon sugar
2 egg chips
1 tablespoon plain yogurt
1 drop vanilla
¼ teaspoon red vinegar

Rectangular Pan

½ teaspoon unsweetened cocoa
¾ teaspoon red food coloring
3 tablespoons cake flour
   (not self-rising)
1 smidgen salt
1 dash baking soda
1 tablespoon butter

1½ tablespoons sugar
3 egg chips
1½ tablespoons plain yogurt
2 drops vanilla
¼ teaspoon red vinegar

Preheat the oven; butter the pan. Mix the cocoa and food coloring in a small cup. In another small cup, mix the flour, salt and baking soda.

Cream the butter and sugar together in your mixing bowl. Add the egg chips, vanilla and cocoa/food coloring mixture and mix well. Add the flour mixture and mix well. Stir in the yogurt and beat one minute. Spread evenly in the pan.

Bake 15 minutes. Frost with cream cheese frosting, page 41.

APPLESAUCE CAKE

Round pan

2 tablespoons all-purpose flour
1 dash baking soda
1 speck salt
1 dash cinnamon
1 speck cloves
1½ teaspoons butter
1 egg chip
1 tablespoon applesauce
1 tablespoon honey or molasses
1 tablespoon raisins

Rectangular pan

3 tablespoons flour
1 dash baking soda
1 speck salt
1 dash cinnamon
1 speck cloves
1 tablespoon butter
2 egg chips
1½ tablespoons applesauce
1½ tablespoons honey or molasses
1½ tablespoons raisins

Preheat the oven and butter the pan.

In your mixing bowl, stir together the flour, baking soda, salt, cinnamon and cloves.

In a separate bowl, mix the butter and egg, then add applesauce and honey or molasses. Mix well. Add the wet mixture to the dry mixture and stir, then beat one minute. Stir in the raisins.

Spread evenly in pan.

Bake 20 minutes.

CHEESECAKE

Graham cracker crust

Round pan

½ teaspoon butter
1 graham cracker square
1 teaspoon sugar

Rectangular pan

2 teaspoons butter
2 graham cracker squares
2 teaspoons sugar

Preheat the oven. Butter and flour the pan

Put the butter in your baking pan and set on top of your oven to melt. Put the graham cracker in a plastic bag and mash with a rolling pin, the back of a spoon or a can until it is all crumbs. Add the sugar, then the melted butter, and knead the bag to mix.

Put this mixture in the pan and press it into a crust covering the bottom of the pan and halfway up the sides. Bake 5 minutes.

Filling

Round pan:

3 tablespoons cream cheese at room temperature
2 teaspoons sugar
2 egg chips
1 teaspoon milk
1 drop vanilla

Rectangular pan

5 tablespoons cream cheese at room temperature
1 tablespoon sugar
3 egg chips
2 teaspoons milk
2 drops vanilla

Mix the filling ingredients together well, then pour into baked crust.

Bake 20 minutes or until set.

Tip: The graham cracker crust is also good for cream pies. Fill the crust with pudding, mix in some cut-up bananas if you like, and top with whipped cream or fruit.

FROSTING

How much do you need?

These recipes will frost one round cake layer. For more, just multiply:

x2 for one rectangular layer
x3 for two round layers
x4 if you cut the rectangular cake into two layers

Hint: Too much frosting is better than too little!

Frosting too stiff? Add milk, a little at a time.

Too thin? Add some powdered sugar.

1) Vanilla Frosting

½ teaspoon butter at room temperature
3 tablespoons powdered sugar
1 drop vanilla
½ teaspoon milk

Cream butter and sugar together. Add vanilla and milk; beat with a fork.

2) Chocolate Frosting

3 tablespoons powdered sugar
1 teaspoon cocoa for light frosting;
2 teaspoons for dark frosting
½ teaspoon butter at room temperature
1 drop vanilla
½ teaspoon milk

Mix sugar with cocoa. Cream butter and sugar mixture together.

Add vanilla and milk and beat with a fork.

3) CREAM CHEESE FROSTING

1 teaspoon cream cheese at room
    temperature
1 teaspoon butter at room
    temperature
3 tablespoons powdered sugar
1 drop vanilla

Mix cheese and butter together, mix thoroughly with sugar and vanilla.

4) GLAZE FOR COOKIES

¼ cup confectioner's sugar
2 teaspoons milk
1 drop vanilla

Mix the three ingredients together until the mixture is nice and smooth.

Variations:
- Use orange juice or half lemon juice, half water instead of milk and vanilla.
- Use another extract instead of vanilla. (Maple extract is terrific.)
- Add a tiny drop of food coloring.

41

Pie Crust

Round pan:

2 tablespoons plus 1 teaspoon
   all-purpose flour
1 smidgen salt
2 teaspoons shortening
1¼ teaspoons water

Rectangular pan:

4 tablespoons all-purpose flour
1 pinch salt

4 teaspoons shortening
2¼ teaspoons water

Preheat oven. Use a little extra shortening to grease the pan. (Usually you don't need to grease a pie pan, but for the toy oven you do.)

Mix the flour and salt in a bowl. Add the shortening and mash it into the flour with the back of a fork. Add the water and mix.

You can roll out the dough with a rolling pin and place in the pan or just press it evenly onto the bottom and sides of the pan with your fingers. Be careful not to let it get too thick where the bottom of the pan meets the sides.

If your recipe requires a prebaked crust, bake 10 minutes.

FRuit Pie

Use any fruit cut into small pieces — no larger than a pea.

Preheat the oven.

Round pan:

An unbaked piecrust
Enough cut-up fruit to fill the pan
1½ teaspoons sugar
1 smidgen cornstarch
4 tablespoons fruit

Rectangular pan:

An unbaked piecrust
Enough cut-up fruit to fill the pan
3 teaspoons sugar
1 dash cornstarch
8 tablespoons fruit

Mix the sugar and cornstarch in a bowl, then mix in the fruit. Spread this mixture in the crust, making sure nothing sticks up higher than the sides of the pan. You can squish it down gently with the back of a spoon. Cram in as much as will fit, but if it's still too high, remove some fruit.

Bake 35 minutes.

COCONUT CUSTARD PIE

Round Pan

A baked pie crust
4 egg chips
2 tablespoons milk
1 teaspoon sugar
1 speck salt
1 drop vanilla
1 tablespoon flaked coconut

Rectangular Pan

A baked pie crust
8 egg chips
4 tablespoons milk
2 tablespoons sugar
1 smidgen salt
2 drops vanilla
2 tablespoons flaked coconut

Preheat the oven.

Mix egg, milk, sugar, salt and vanilla. Break up any clumps in coconut and add that. Place your pan with the crust close to the oven, then pour the filling into pie crust. Spread the coconut evenly. Put your pan into the oven carefully so nothing spills.

Bake 20 minutes, or until filling is set.

"WHAT'S THAT...?"

SET: the filling isn't liquid any more; the egg has cooked and solidified just as it does when you make scrambled eggs.

44

PUMPKiN PiE

Pumpkin pie is just a custard pie with pumpkin mixed in. You can use canned pumpkin in the following recipe, but if you are making a jack-o-lantern for Halloween, you can use the pieces you cut out to make the eyes, nose and mouth.

Cooked pumpkin for pie:

Eyes, mouth and nose from jack-o-lantern

Preheat the oven; butter the pan. Pare the skin from the pieces of pumpkin and cut the pumpkin flesh into smaller pieces that will fit in your pan. Put as many pieces as you can into the pan without letting any be higher than the rim. Bake 20 minutes. Cool a few minutes, then mash thoroughly with a fork.

You need a sharp knife for this. Ask an adult for help!

To make the pie:

Round pan

A baked pie crust
2 egg chips
1 tablespoon sugar
1 dash cinnamon
1 speck of each: ginger, nutmeg, allspice, cloves

46

1 tablespoon cooked, mashed
    pumpkin (or canned pumpkin)
1 tablespoon milk

Rectangular pan

A baked pie crust
4 egg chips
2 tablespoons sugar
¼ teaspoon cinnamon
1 speck of each: ginger, nutmeg,
    allspice, cloves
2 tablespoons cooked, mashed
pumpkin (or canned pumpkin)
2 tablespoons milk

Preheat the oven.

Mix sugar and spices together. Mix eggs, pumpkin and milk, then add sugar and spices. Place your pan halfway in the oven slot, then pour mixture into crust. Push the pan slowly into the oven.

Bake 25 minutes, or until filling is set.

What about those pumpkin seeds?

You can even toast the pumpkin seeds in your toy oven. Preheat the oven, clean off any stringy stuff from the seeds, then spread them in the pan.

Bake 20 minutes. When they're cool, peel off the shells and eat. They taste great!

Pecan Pie

Round pan

A baked pie crust
¼ teaspoon butter
1 tablespoon corn syrup
    (light or dark)
3 egg chips
1 tablespoon sugar
1 drop vanilla
4 teaspoons chopped pecans

Rectangular pan

A baked pie crust
½ teaspoon butter
2 tablespoons corn syrup
    (light or dark)
6 egg chips
2 tablespoons sugar
2 drops vanilla
3 tablespoons chopped pecans

Preheat oven.

Put the butter in your mixing bowl and set on top of the oven to melt. Mix in the syrup, eggs, sugar and vanilla, then stir in the pecans. Pour into the pie shell.

Bake 30 minutes.

QUiCHE LoRRaine

Round pan

A baked pie crust
3 egg chips
1½ tablespoons milk
1 speck salt
½ slice cooked bacon
2 teaspoons Swiss cheese cut into small pieces
½ teaspoon grated Parmesan or
    Romano cheese

Rectangular pan

A baked pie crust
6 egg chips
3 tablespoons milk
1 smidgen salt
1 slice cooked bacon
1 tablespoon Swiss cheese cut
    into small pieces
1 teaspoon grated Parmesan or
    Romano cheese

Mix the eggs, milk and salt. Crumble the bacon and spread over the crust. Spread the cheese evenly over the bacon. Place your pan close to the oven and pour the egg-milk mixture into it. Put your pan into the oven carefully so nothing spills out.

Bake 25 minutes, or until filling is set.

APPLE BROWN BETTY

Round Pan

1 teaspoon butter
4 teaspoons white bread torn
   into small pieces
1 teaspoon brown sugar
1 smidgen cinnamon
2 tablespoons very small, thin
   pieces of apple

Rectangular Pan

2 teaspoons sugar
3 tablespoons white bread torn
   into small pieces
2 teaspoons brown sugar
1 pinch cinnamon
4 tablespoons very small, thin
   pieces of apple
Preheat the oven.

Put the butter in your baking pan and place on top of the oven to melt. Add the bread to the melted butter and swish it around so it soaks up the butter.

Mix the brown sugar and cinnamon, then add the apples.

Add the apple mixture to the bread and butter and stir around in the pan so that some of the bread is on top.

Bake 30 minutes.

Yeast Bread

Round Pan

½ teaspoon butter
1 tablespoon water
¼ teaspoon fast-rising yeast
¼ teaspoon sugar
1 smidgen salt
1 tablespoon milk
3 tablespoons all-purpose flour

Rectangular Pan

¾ teaspoon butter
1 tablespoon water
¼ teaspoon fast-rising yeast
¼ teaspoon sugar
1 pinch salt
2 tablespoons milk
5 tablespoons all-purpose flour

Preheat oven. Put butter in small bowl and set on top of oven to melt.

Mixing:

Put water in mixing bowl, sprinkle yeast on top, let stand five minutes. When butter is melted, add it to the water and yeast mixture with sugar, salt and milk. (Don't wash the butter-melting cup yet.) Add flour and stir until it forms a ball. Leave it alone 10 minutes.

Kneading:

Put some flour on your very clean hands and start playing with the ball of dough. Pull it apart; it will break, sort of like PlayDoh. Now squeeze it and roll it in your hands. Smash it, stretch it — whatever you want. After a few minutes it will get smoother, less sticky and more stretchy, more like Silly Putty.

First Rising:
Put the dough ball in the cup that still has some melted butter in it. Roll the dough around to coat it with butter on all sides. Cover with plastic wrap. Put a folded dishtowel or potholder on top of the oven and put the cup of dough on top. Leave it alone for 30 minutes.

Second Rising:
The dough should have risen to about double by now. Poke it with your finger. It will make a hole that doesn't bounce back.

Butter the baking pan.

Put the dough in the baking pan and squash it down, spreading it to the edge of the pan. Cover with plastic wrap and put on the towel on top of the oven. Leave it alone for 30 minutes.

Baking:
By now the dough should have risen enough to bake. If it sticks up over the edge of the pan, pat the high spots very gently to even with the pan.

Bake 20 minutes.

To cook the hamburgers:

Preheat the oven. Using your table-spoon, scoop 3 balls of meat for the round pan or 6 balls for the rectangular pan. Flatten each ball into a patty; sprinkle each side with a little salt and pepper and place in pan.

Bake 15 minutes.

To make cheeseburgers, cut a piece of American cheese 1" x 1" and put on top of cooked hamburger. Be careful to keep everything lower than the side of the pan. Put back in oven for two minutes. Put on buns and add ketchup or your favorite toppings.

Tip: Always wash your hands after handling raw meat.

To make the buns:

Take the heels (ends) from a loaf of white bread. Place the bread on a cutting board or plate with the dark side up. Use a cookie cutter or bottle cap about 1½ inches in diameter to cut rounds from the bread. You'll need 6 for the round pan or 12 for the rectangular pan.

Baked Custard

Round pan

4 egg chips
4 tablespoons milk
1 teaspoon sugar
1 drop vanilla
1 speck salt
1 smidgen nutmeg

Rectangular pan

7 egg chips
7 tablespoons milk
2 teaspoons sugar
2 drops vanilla
1 speck salt
1 dash nutmeg

Preheat the oven and butter the pan.

A measuring cup or small pitcher makes a good mixing bowl for this recipe. Mix the eggs, milk, sugar, vanilla and salt.

Beat one minute with a fork. Put the pan halfway into the oven slot. Carefully pour the mixture into the pan. Sprinkle the nutmeg on top and swish it around with a knife so it is distributed over the top of the egg mixture. Now, slowly push the pan into the oven.

Bake 15 minutes.

Chill in refrigerator before you eat it.

55

Round pan

2 tablespoons all-purpose flour
1 dash baking powder
1 pinch salt
1 teaspoon olive oil
2 teaspoons water

Rectangular pan

4 tablespoons all-purpose flour
¼ teaspoon baking powder
1 dash salt
2 teaspoons olive oil
4 teaspoons water

Mix flour, baking powder and salt, then add olive oil and water.

With your fingers, pat dough evenly in pan and up the sides. Continue with pizza recipe on page 58.

Yeast CRust FOR Pizza

Round pan

¼ teaspoon fast-rising yeast
2 teaspoons water
¼ teaspoon sugar
1 pinch salt
½ teaspoon olive oil
2 tablespoons all-purpose flour

Rectangular pan

½ teaspoon fast-rising yeast
4 teaspoons water
½ teaspoon sugar
1 dash salt
1 teaspoon olive oil
4 tablespoons all-purpose flour

Sprinkle the yeast on top of the water in your mixing bowl. After five minutes, add the sugar, salt and oil. Add the flour, mix well, then leave it alone ten minutes.

Follow the directions on page 52 for kneading and first rising, but use olive oil in the rising cup instead of butter.

After the dough has risen for thirty minutes, you can use it without a second rising. Just use your fingers to pat it evenly into the pan and up the sides.

Continue with the pizza recipe on page 58.

Pizza

Round pan

An unbaked pizza crust from
    page 56
1 tablespoon pizza sauce
2 tablespoons shredded mozzarella
    cheese
1 teaspoon toppings of your choice

Rectangular pan

An unbaked pizza crust from
    page 56
3 tablespoons pizza sauce

4 tablespoons shredded mozzarella
    cheese
1 tablespoon toppings of your choice

Preheat the oven.

Spread the sauce evenly on the crust.
Sprinkle cheese on top, then add
toppings if you are using them.
Pat the top with your fingers to make
sure everything is below the edge of
the pan.

Bake 40 minutes.

Toppings can include small bits of
pepperoni or cooked Italian sausage,
onion, peppers, oregano, etc.

Liver & Lima Bean PUDDING

Just kidding! You won't find a recipe for liver and lima bean pudding here, but I'll bet there is such a thing and it might even taste good. People have always experimented with new combinations and methods. Some of them work, some don't. Now that you know the basics of baking, you can use those principles to invent new recipes. If you come up with something wonderful, I'd love to hear about it.

You also might want to try some full-sized recipes. You'll find plenty online or in cookbooks you probably already have in your house. Wouldn't it be great to surprise your brother or sister with a homemade birthday cake or make a coffee cake for your parents' anniversary breakfast?

Happy Baking & Happy Eating!

INDEX

9 781944 037086